ASCENDANCE

D1496411

ASCENDANCE

POEMS BY
TIM MCNULTY

Pleasure Boat Studio
New York

Second Printing

Pleasure Boat Studio: A Literary Press
201 West 89th Street
New York, NY 10024
Tel/Fax 413-677-0085
www.pleasureboatstudio.com/pleasboat@nyc.rr.com

ISBN 978–1–929355–93–8
Library of Congress Control Number 2013904313

Cover image: *Salmon Ascending Kettle Falls, Washington.* Historic photograph by Ellis Morigeau, used with permission from the Teakle Collection, Northwest Room, Spokane Public Library.
Book design by Greg Darms.

FOR CAITLIN

ACKNOWLEDGEMENTS

Grateful acknowledgement is made to the editors and publishers of these publications in which some of these poems first appeared:

MAGAZINES:
Clover, A Literary Rag; Drawn to the Light; Duckabush Journal; Floating Bridge Review; International Writers Workshop; Kingfisher; Lived Experience (Canada)*; The Moment Witnessed; The Sound Close In; Mountain Gazette; Moving Mountain; Nisqually Delta Review; Northwind; Origin; Potlatcxh; Raven Chronicles; Seattle Metropolitan Magazine; Spiritually Fit.com; Vigilance; Wilderness Magazine;* and *Windfall;*

ANTHOLOGIES:
Fast Moving Water, Documentary Media, Seattle, 2008; *Working the Woods, Working the Sea,* Empty Bowl, Port Townsend, 2008; *In the Blast Zone,* Oregon State University Press, Corvallis, 2008; *River of Memory,* University of Washington Press, 2006; *A Writers Harvest of Poetry,* Peninsula College, Port Angeles, 1997; *Padilla Bay Poets Anthology,* Padilla Bay Foundation, Mt. Vernon, 2006; *Hands Joining,* Brooding Heron Press, Waldron Island, 1988.

BROADSIDES:
"The Counsel of Pines" by Woodland Pattern Book Center, Milwaukee, 2010; "Some Ducks" by Tangram Press, Berkeley, 2008; "Night, Sourdough Mountain Lookout" by Egress Studio, Bellingham, 2005; "Short Songs for the Spring Peepers" by Longhouse, Vermont, 1997.

CHAPBOOKS:
Some Ducks, Pleasure Boat Studio, New York, 2009; *Through High Still Air,* Pleasure Boat Studio, New York, 2005; *Reflected Light,* Tangram Press, Berkeley, 1990.

CONTENTS

‹ 1 ›
SOME DUCKS

A Cycle of Poems for my Daughter

FIRST SONG

As I started up the gravel drive
in the early hours
       to meet you,
a breathlike mist covered the field,
and a crescent moon
  —near-edge
         of a pearl—

    floated free

from the dark limbs of a fir tree.

CAITLIN AND THE MOON

Just days old,
we take you to visit friends in the valley.

Driving home now, in darkness,
the rounding moon drifts west
       toward the mountains
           like a boatful of light.

Asleep in your mother's arms,
the moonlight wakes you.

I watch your small face,
eyes wide to this strange new light,
       as you watch.

The moon follows us through the trees,
lighting narrow fields
that rise into darkened foothills.

For the first time,
your dreamy gaze fastens to something
other than your mother or me,
something full and luminous
and curiously alive.

And it seems that an understanding
passes between you—earth being
and heavenly lamp—an assurance
       pure and necessary as milk.

At home, by the river,
bundled into a wicker bassinet,
for the first time you sleep
            through the night.

And your cry at first light
is as small and bright
        as a birdsong.

CAITLIN AND THE BEAR

My daughter had nearly passed the tree
by the time I noticed it: a mossy cedar
with the buttressed swell of its base
stripped clean to bright sapwood;
shreds of ripped bark and woodchips
scattered over the trail like leaves.

"Caitlin," I called, "Who ate that?"
She stopped and her gaze climbed
to the claw-torn edge of bark
higher than me. And she:
"Somebody big."

We felt the wiggly tracks
of beetle larvae,
powder-filled furrows in the orange wood,
and the claw marks raked across them.

"Somebody," I said,
"must have been awfully hungry."
And Caitlin, as if suddenly
looking up at one across the dinner table,
sang out, *"A bear!"*
And then, just as quickly, "Where is it?"

So we looked,
through ferns, out past the tall columns
of trees, behind us . . .
"He must have wandered off," I said;
then, catching her mother's quick glance, added
"a few weeks ago."

We should have known that later
she would find him,
a shadowy figure among the ferns
that looked to us like a stump.
But we all kept right on walking anyway,
just in case.

THE BRIGHTNESS

—for Caitlin and Trisha

My daughter and her friend hold hands
in low breaking swells
on a pebble beach at the edge of the world.

Black oystercatchers dash
noisily over the waves
and gulls idle along the tideline,
hands clasped behind them
      like bank guards.

All the teller windows are open.

The girls jump and shiver as cold waves
break against legs and bellies.
Their silhouettes dance
in the brightness
      lithe and diminutive as waterbugs.

As the largest
of small waves approaches,
Caitlin, the younger, pulls free, wanting
      to catch it by herself.

How well I know that gesture.

"We're floating backwards!"
they scream, as outwash
sucks at their ankles and
buries their shiny feet in sand.
The illusion
      pitches them off-balance.

When the dads at last give in
and walk out to join them: it's true.

Waves splinter into diamonds
at our feet, and,
heavy with sunlight and sand,
sweep away
          the years between us.

I whirl and plunge
an awkward half-step back
for balance, and shout:
"We're floating backwards!"
          too.

PONCHO IN HEAVEN

1

I don't know what sent your kitty
bounding across the road
just then.
Maybe a redwing blackbird
whistling the evening light across the pond,
or the marsh wren it chases
through the cattail reeds.

When I listen to the redwing's song now,
I can almost hear the answer
of Poncho's bell
as he leaps from the long roadside grass
into forever.

2

For Poncho, the cars and trucks and noise
no longer exist. And bright
wingbeats flash among the cattails
like jewels.
It is always that wide and hopeful moment
before the bird hears the small bell
muffled in fur
and springs from its bowed stem
into the open field of sky.

In that moment, the sky
is Poncho's, too, as he sails
over the gold-green spring grass,
light as thistledown,
farther than you or I can see.

3

In your drawing,
you hold Poncho close to your chest,
while another Poncho
—the same soft gray on white
with bushy black tail—
floats above you.

In your simple working of crayon,
and paste, you've made something beautiful,
a fresco of holding and letting go,

an image of a timeless present
where all we know of love
and loss
spills past the words
                    we have to tell it.

WILD ANIMALS

Dinner over, just past dark,
and my daughter refuses
to carry out the compost.
"There's wild animals out there."

"That's nonsense," I say, grabbing the pail
and purposely
leaving the flashlight behind.
Past the porch light,
total darkness.
Then, just beside me,
a deer startles
and jumps noisily into the brush.

A dozen steps later, heart still hammering,
I lean to tip the pail, and a low
toothy snarl rises from darkness
a foot away.
I'm halfway back to the house,
compost scattered, before I realize . . .
raccoon.

"Christ!"
as the kitchen door slams behind me:
"There's wild animals out there."

The Pope of Swimming Bear Lake

Three years ago, waiting out some
                        rainy weather,
I camped by this small mountain tarn.
It was your fifth birthday, and
guilty for dodging the party,
I wrote this story for you
in my journal:

        A long time ago, before
        even I was born,
        a black bear went swimming
        in the blue snowmelt water
                of this lake.

        I know this because
        a mountain man named Crisler
        filmed that old bear
        and put him in a movie.

        Crisler filmed from high
        on the ridge, and the bear
        looked like he was dancing
        —floating in air—over blue-green
                lakebottom stones.

        That's what gave the lake
        its name.

Because you love bears so much—and own
no fewer than ten of them—
I wanted you to have this story,
so when you finally came here yourself
you'd know this place
                    as an old friend.

How could I have known
you'd make your way here so soon?
And the two bears you found here today,
flipping over rocks on the steep slope
                    (hungry for ants and grubs)
would give you your own story.

All night, the rains wash
against our tent fly,
and the muffled clack of boulders
tumble through the darkness.

Morning, we follow an elk trail
across a steep open slope.
The black bear who meets us
        (and doesn't really want to leave
        his berry patch to let us by—
                    but finally does)
is way wetter than us.

He leans on his elbows
on a tuft of sedge, scruffy ears and dark
                    shiny nose,
and peers down at us, questioningly.

I'm not sure what to say
when you hold up your Hiking Bear
to show him we're friends.

He seems to squint,
like I do sometimes at the newspaper.
But all the news is good.
He slips lazily back into a swale,
and we stroll on by in our shiny, wet rain suits
                    proud as bishops
blessed by an audience with the Pope.

14

SOME DUCKS

"Now, if we're real quiet . . . ," I whisper to Caitlin,

and with the next step
a thunder of wings fills the sky,
cloudburst of feathers and spray
as dozens of mallards explode
               from the small pond.
Blue-white shimmer of wingbars and vapor
billows across the winter sky.

Caitlin stands frozen,
as a second, then third wave
               erupts before us,
astonished
that our quiet approach
could trigger such spectacular alarm.

The roiled surface splashes up in waves
over the shore ice,
the din of wingbeats fades,
and the sky is suddenly
               monumental in its emptiness.

Our eyes meet with my unfinished thought:

" . . . we might see some ducks."

State Championship

"There is another great joy in this.
There is the dancer,
and there is the one singing for the dancer."
    —Robert Sund

The gym is cacophonous, girls
in sweats and leotards everywhere;
four events—floor, beam, uneven bars,
the calamitous hurdle—
all running at once,
and kitschy music crackles through the air
like tinfoil.

You stand in the midst of it all,
poised and attentive,
awaiting a nod from the judges
        to begin.

                Then,
stepping forward on the mat
in measured paces,
you suddenly
        leap
                like a waterbird,
and spring, cartwheeling into a round-off,
flip mid-air,
                a blur of arms and legs,
        and land
                gracefully
arms raised, a toe
                pointed gingerly forward,
        pause and begin again.

16

Somewhere, in the strict forms
       and months of training,
you've found the freedom to take flight.

Parents and friends clap and shake our heads
in disbelief; your teammates cheer,
and the judges smile approvingly.

       But your focus is elsewhere.

Facing around and taking a long breath,
you launch into a dizzying crescendo
       of leaps, tucks, back handsprings and flips
             —hands and feet drumming the mat—
       and again, the graceful, dancelike skip
and landing to an eruption of applause.

I saw in your eyes
            in that moment's pause
       the wild mixture of joy
           and fierce determination
that pushes the spirit outward
       through toned and practiced limbs
            to a newer emanation of itself—
       fleet and beautiful and wholly
              self-contained.

Alone and joyous amid the noise and chaos
of the world reeling around you.

GRASSHOPPERS

Warm autumn hillside
above the low song
         of a dwindling river;
     sharp *clack-clack-clack*
of grasshoppers
      whapping their wings
      over the dry grass and boulders.

Brief flash of yellow and gray
disappears into dust.

I think: "band-wings," but can't be sure.

If my daughter were here
she would surely have caught one by now.
It would loom,
        dinosaur-like in our handlens,
        waving its short horns,
    and we'd know the species.

But even now, I feel
her lifetime of catch-and-release
       nature study
is about to strike out in a new
      —and frightening—direction,

leaving me, the bugs and the rocks
    to ourselves.

Winter Solstice: Moonrise at Century's End

With my daughter,
I drive the old pickup
to the top of Lost Mountain
              for the big event.
We kick down the tailgate,
spread out blankets,
pour licorice tea from a thermos
and wait.

Below us, Puget Sound and the straits
are shrouded in a blanket of their own.
In the chill darkness,
Caitlin thinks water at first,
then sees: a sea of cloud.

It laps the shore of nearby hills
in improbably slow waves of mist,
breaks against headlands,
floods inlets, making bays of creeks
and draws, swallows
              islands of trees.

We're cold. It's dark. When finally,
a small band of opalescent light
traces the eastern horizon. Then,
like the visitation of an archangel,
a great yellow globe ascends
beyond the Cascade peaks.

It is so clear
we can see the moon's ragged edge
roughened with contours, its face
pocked with craters,

textured extravagantly with shadow
and light.

As the orb drifts free of the mountains
it lights the sea of cloud
for a hundred miles.
Deep swells, rolling breakers,
bottomless canyons stir
slow and restless as tides
                    in the moonlight.

After a time, Caitlin asks
"Why don't we do this every night?"
Her cheeks are flushed with cold;
moonlight glints in her eyes.
If I tell her the truth,
what will she think of me?

DIVERS

Before practice the divers walk
on their hands along the far edge of the pool.

Their reflections in the still, blue water
merge with their actual selves,
palm to palm,
hand-stepping delicately along the curb
like mythic creatures—half liquid,
half vapor, long-limbed and angelic—
feeling their way
along the verge of earthly elements.

In minutes they will hurl themselves
swanlike through the unhurried air,
spin like tumbler pigeons
and rip the clear surface water
sleek and powerful as dolphins.

But now, as the girls move delicately
as water striders, bound neither by earth
nor gravity nor time, they are most themselves.

Balanced and playful in the grace
of their bodies, they are masters
of colliding elements,
hand walkers on the liquid lip
of the possible,

acrobats of the air who have yet to show us
how much can be accomplished
in a few brief seconds of flight.

⟩ 2 ⟩
REFLECTED LIGHT

Poems on Paintings by Morris Graves

JOYOUS YOUNG PINES

—for Morris Graves

On a grassy terrace
above the sedge
      and willow-crowded flat
where Owl Creek
threads its chilly way east
from the hills,

lodgepole pine seedlings
lift curved limbs
into the first rays of sunlight
as if to shake off
      a heavy evening frost,

as if breathing the light
through thousands
of thin-needled leaves,
      each
saying, *yes . . . yes!*
in the eloquent chemistry
of their quiet speech.

"Varied Thrush Calling in Autumn"

The earth
is a page of dark-washed browns,
where a bough and needles
        riffle in tense wind.

A dozen brushstrokes
give life to
        the shape of a bird in song.

Its single pure note
        in a season darkening with war
forms a broad wingshape of hope
                which contains it.

Bird, wind and season:
        the quiet flight of music
                sweetened
        by the coming cold.

"Resilient Young Pine"

Wind has emptied
half the sky
and the sapling boughs
      are bent
           and swept back with it,

the young tree drawn
      tense as a fist,
yet holding in its palm
          a stillness.

This gesture:
the whipped limbs and
          threadlike lacework
      of needles
—undaunted beauty
      of life holding forth—
gives grace to the storm
          that shapes it.

"JOYOUS YOUNG PINE"

The flushed glow of new life
hidden in bud
      and early gold-green leafage
quickens a young pine
      with a thousand warm
          and radiant leaves.

It's the spring of its
          fourth year.
Shallow roots deepen
      in the temperate earth,
and a smooth skein of bark
sheathes its stem.

There is a sureness
         and steadiness now,
     first days after budburst;
a springing upward
      out of the ground of being.

And pale golden roselight,
        an alpenglow of birth,
     lights the world.

"Shore Birds Submerged in Moonlight"

Moonlight
in mist at the water's edge
is a calligraphy
        of blue-white brushstrokes.

Only faintly
the heads of shorebirds
        —wide eyes and long
                slender beaks—
peer out past tideline
toward a heaving and restless sea.

It is 1940.
The moonlight has given them shape:
small birds
        clustered at land's end
as the ocean breaks over turbulent depths
                of gray and black
the painter has only hinted at.

"EACH TIME YOU CARRY ME THIS WAY"

For you and I have been both,
carrier and carried, hunter
and prey,
in our time among moonlit water.

Though the distance from shore
to shore lessens
with each passage, always
the quiet bird waits
attentive in the shallows
at perception's edge.

I woke one frostlit night
by a stream in a northern range,
the stillness pierced
by an owl's call
that cut the dream of time like a blade.

Stars held motionless,
the night grew large;
and who I was
about to become
called from a portal of darkened trees.

   *"Every time
   I carry you this way . . . "*

—Vishnu to the goddess Earth,
the first dawn of the Yuga—

Dawn breaks forever
where a bird stands
bowed at the edge of the world.

The self is a hidden radiance there,
gleaned from the depths:
a small fish
caught and carried into light.

"HIBERNATION" I

The earth rolls quietly
in cool, dark waves
beneath a burning sky.

A single pulse of her being
reaches down
to encircle a small, sleeping animal.

Curled, its small face
against legs, it is almost self-
contained. And would be, but

for its tail—
that last trapping
of physical being.

It sweeps back
into the rolling earth,
still and forever part of that motion
from which the sleeping form
takes its rest.

"HIBERNATION" II

The washed ink of winter
or night
encloses the page.

In its center
a small stripe-tailed mammal sleeps
tucked in a perfect sphere.

Brushstrokes trace
a shadowed, downturned face
—closed eyes, whiskers,
        the dark tip of a nose—

and the roundling motion
of its curved tail is echoed
with a luminous sweep of light

that holds the sleeping body
inviolate,
as light holds all of form
and matter at its heart.

"Hibernation" III

1

In soft, mottled earth
beneath the hedgerows
                    and leaves
of memory and perception,
a small animal sleeps curled
in the shape of an egg.

Its warmth
forms an embryo of soft
            muted light,
as if the darkened earth
                    were a womb,
as though
beneath the dust and clutter
                    of consciousness,
        being
and being born
                    were one.

2

Alongside
and overlapping the sleeping form,
centered just beyond
        the small closed eyes,

the luminescent glow of awareness:

a double-hued mandala of light
almost overpowering
                in its brilliance.

Here, held apart, but part of
        the body,
the transcendent presence
                of Mind—
of birth and death,
        and of what lies awake
                beyond them.

3

Within the small, clever
mammalian mind,
in stillness,
a soft, steady light
burns beside us.

We carry this vision
inside like a seed,
the shape
of a cell in mitosis.

While we sleep
the quiet measured sleep
between seasons or worlds,
we share
the shape of ourselves
with the perfect
                    spherical shape
          of light.

In the mandala
of the animal body, these
godlike forms drawn
          from the mineral earth,
the small closed eyes
                    are lit from within.

‣3‣
SHOOTING STARS

ABOVE HOH VALLEY

1

In the late slant of mountain light,
    a silver ribbon follows after itself.
River music lifts
    through spruce and hemlock
        a mile below.

2

A low sea of cloud
    hems the foothills
while a finger of mist
    sifts past the first swells of mountain,
        drifts upstream.

3

Along a furrow
    in a sandstone wall,
the slightest star-shaped flower
    steals something from the southern sky.

4

Snow trickles into a still pool;
    a sheet of glass
        widens across the stars.

SHOOTING STARS

Dodecatheon jeffreyi

Midway up the rocky knoll
the slope rises in a shallow ledge of granite.
A skirt of moss
drapes one knobby knee,
and a sunlit ramp of spring grass
ushers me on.

Stepping around bristly moss
        and treading lightly over sedges and grass,
I pull myself to the top of the outcrop
and lean back on sun-warmed stone.

A thick bed of moss at my feet
        is fed by a pool of snowmelt,
and scattered over it,
            a hidden constellation
      of shooting stars.

Their bright, upswept, rose-purple blossoms
        fill the shallow lap of rock
           like comets
    in a mossy heaven.

All winter they lay
enfolded in cold darkness, awaiting
        these first sunlit days

when some nearsighted astronomer
of minutia
        might stumble upon them, and,
           delighted, chart
their brief trajectories of light.

40

LEISURE

Late spring,
I sit on the porch with a cup of wine
watching the wild rhododendrons
unfold in the rain.
Their color, blushed rose in bud, a pale
washed pink in blossom,
is the perfect counterpoint
to the subdued greens of the forest.
Beside them,
the bright ornamental shrubs in town
appear coarse and garish,
though I try to be unbiased in these matters;
it's difficult, given the leisure
to consider them fully.

Late afternoon, a vagrant shaft
of sunlight illumines a young maple
at the far edge of the pasture.
It is as though a shy
and awkward girl
had just stepped forth into womanhood.
Even the birds fall speechless,
though little enough
they've had to sing about
these past five weeks of rain.

SHORT SONGS FOR THE SPRING PEEPERS

Pseudacris regilla

Most years, it's the white
tassels of Indian plum blossoms
turn back winter.

But this year, and last,
the songs of the treefrogs.

⸱

Spring mountain night
bursts awake with a thousand voices.

Treefrogs looking for friends.

⸱

My daughter loves catching them,
hates letting them go.

In the darkened cave of her
          cupped hands,
those wide, copper-gold eyes.

⸱

Sound of a midnight truck
grinding up the mountain road
and the treefrogs fall silent.

We wake into absence of their singing,
like stepping off into a ditch.

⸱

42

Ice still rimes the pond-edge
and the valley grows white with frost.

But the treefrogs are having none of it.

     ,

After love, the storm
      of our breathing subsides
into a deafening chorus of frogs.

Were they there all that time?

     ,

I tell Caitlin
the sticky pads on their
        tiny white toes

are for hugs.

     ,

Asleep beneath a warm
      forest-green quilt,
they coax our dreams

out into the dark wet hollows.

     ,

Full moon
     over a late-season fall of snow.

A single treefrog
cannot contain himself.

     ,

Breathing your warmth,
the light hair at the back
of your neck.

I know what they're saying,
the treefrogs.

　　　　　,

In daylight, they change hue,
meld with whatever shade surrounds them
as easily as a congressman.

　　　　　,

There's a flatter, single-note song
for rainy summer days
　　　　　　　　after mating season,

but no one seems to listen.

A BEAR COMES TO THE WEDDING

—after Howard McCord,
for Richard & Sara

"In this poem
a bear comes to the wedding."

He's lumbered down from the high meadows
fat, shaggy and smelling of musty old logs.

He grins dreamily and mingles with the crowd.
The knees of his pants are grass-stained
and his tie is spotted with berry juice.

The guests pretend not to notice
as he dips a paw gingerly into the potato salad
or orders a raw salmon with his drink.
We all recognize him.

He is the Emissary
from the land beyond the shopping malls,
Senator from the chamber of mossy trees,
Spokesman for the vast and wild realm
we stepped from only yesterday.

He's here to bless the wedding
and kiss the bride, to laugh
and dance with everybody's wife!

He is that large, warm-hearted part of ourselves
that grows euphoric in the presence of love.
If we show him a good time
he just might stay forever.

PLUNGING INTO THE WILD

The tracks led up a snowfield
from Queets Basin to the windy gap
of Dodwell-Rixon Pass,
then stretched out
                as the bear
loped down the Elwha Snowfinger
—claws like crampons in the frozen crust—
and launched
        a steep, hell-bent, belly-sliding
                glissade,
a joyous plunge into the wild
headwaters of the Elwha.

Not one to question the protocols
of a mountain god,
I let loose a *whoop*
            and plunge after.

THUNDER AT LENA LAKE

—for Mary

By midday the low rumble of thunder
had built to a storm.
We watched the charged air whiten
with sheets of rain
and the dark lakewater boil.

Lunch was short that day,
and the steep climb to the upper lake
a wet one.
All afternoon we followed the dashed
and swollen stream,
crossing on slippery boulders.

By evening the clouds had lifted some,
and Upper Lena was empty
and still.

There's something about thunder
always draws me out into it,
a sharpness in the electric air
and the cool wet calm that follows.

I said
the lower lake was like the world
that waits back at road's end,
so wrapped in its storm there is nothing else.

You said, that's why we climb.

A pair of mountain chickadees
chipped tentatively

from a cluster of alpine firs.
We'll make some tea
and watch the mists roll back,
you and me,
with damp sweaters and soggy boots,
and no more plans than that.

METHOW VALLEY FALL

1

At noon
shapes of deer
browse the fog at the edge
            of an autumn meadow.
Their tall, spindly ears
        listen backward
to hear what I might have in mind.

2

Later,
tufts of gold-brown bunch grass
        line the dark trail.
Yarrow stalks, scarlet buckwheat,
        spindle-brown leaves of serviceberry
            twirl in mountain wind.

3

In a darkened glade
        beneath crowded firs,
the last gold coins
            of maple leaves
fall into an open palm.

THREE TETON POEMS

With No Song

Evening in the Tetons,
a single cloud trails north
from the summit,
and the broken walls are etched sharply
in a low angle of light.

All night
the canyon will sing
the same song to itself,
and wind will curl
about the ridges and towers
with nothing to promise,

with no song it hasn't sung
for an epoch or two
and nothing new in its pocket
but a handful of sand.

In the Burrow of Night

Early fall on Owl Creek,
the stars step slowly across the valley
and frost circles the tent.
A great gray owl barks and
hoots up the pine woods,
first west of camp, then closer north,
then back.

Waking in the moonless dark,
I am, for a moment, a small
pocket gopher or hare—some
long-lingering mammalian kin—
and burrow down into my bag
'against the chill,' I tell myself.

Frost

Somehow the delicate
evening sky blue petals
of roundleaf bluebells survive
the thick evening frost
unscathed
and nod only slightly
to the dew-drenched morning,
where even the tough
old sagebrush limbs
bow to it.

THE DEAL

I woke shivering,
the fire out, and saw
in dark overcast

the shape of Raven,
big as a dog, tugging
the straps of my pack.

I half rose, tried
to shout but
sputtered, couldn't
speak, could
barely breathe . . .

Look, said Raven,
here's the deal.
I let you kick right now,
or you let me
see what you've got here.

Fell back numbly with
long shuddering breaths.

Woke again
at first light, a fine
mistlike rain. All

I thought I had
scattered
over wet ground.

Two China Poems

Wild Pears

> *Pyrus serotina*

At the waterfall gorge
in Tai Lam Chung Valley,
Ka-shiang brings
      a sprig of wild pears.

Fruits no bigger than mountain berries,
but sweet and chewy—
same taste as the crisp
Asian pears
from the market at Kowloon Tong

where each small globe is wrapped
        in delicate paper mesh . . .

only wilder.

The Cormorant Fisherman

Too old and frail
to fish his bamboo boat
                on the Li River,
he waits
with his cormorants
      perched
on their bamboo pole
              by the pier
for the tour boats from Guilin.

POEM WITH A GOOD BEGINNING

Making a living, what the hell,
a raccoon's got to take a chance now and then.
So broad daylight he steps
off the porch and pirouettes past the window
where I sit blankly at my desk.

Humped shoulders, scrawny wrists,
and that preposterous mask. A good
three times the size of the cat—who's
not small—he disappears around a corner
smug as you please.

I don't have to get up
to know what the compost pile will look like
in five minutes.
I don't have to get up at all,
so I don't, but sit there knowing
the odds are against us both
at least half the time.

UP SHIT CREEK

—for Robert Sund

The low sun has settled
into the small fir trees of Bald Island,
and a cool upriver wind
has nudged back the heat of the day.

Out on the wooden dock
you wash up some greens
for supper.
A few leaves drift
on the incoming tide;
a cliff swallow glints overhead.

Not an idle bug lingers
over the dark water,
but a fish flops anyway,
like a hopeful poet
reaching into an empty pocket
for change.

THREE POEMS FOR DENISE LEVERTOV

1

Pear boughs, pruned
late in season,
the twig-ends knotted with buds.

Gathered to indoor warmth
and water, they swell
loose and begin to open—

offer blossoms
that will never bear fruit.

As though that sharp
sever from the whole
were little more than dream.

Cut limbs
flowering on a sunlit shelf:

white petals,
grayed wood.

2

Pawtracks
small on cold white earth,

past a woodbock
and gnarled pear,
the empty shed open—

something gone.

A wind that froze the pipes,
an ash-wet sky,
and tracks

off through the first snow.

3

What the sun does
off behind the snow mountains
when it goes there

no one knows, but
it must be something wonderful,
something that transforms,

making all of heaven throb
pulse-red and the seas burn,
as if it were

pleased with its children,
or displeased, or more
that we,

now losing sight
of its presence
are given

a brief glimpse
of the power of its gift.

LIGHTS OF THE VALLEY

—for Mick and Christie Nelson,
Pipestone Canyon, Christmas Eve, 1985

The wind sifts powder snow
down through the clefts and grottos
of cliffy canyon walls,
and the small pines darken
into evening.

Where the canyon narrows
            and steepens at its head,
we take off our skis
and follow the frozen tracks of horses
to a low pass.

Beyond a gate and slackwire fence,
silhouetted against a snowy rise,
the small band of horses
huddles against an aspen grove.

The bare trees offer little shelter,
and mountain winds stiffen
with the coming dark.
For a time,
they perk their ears and watch
as we stomp warmth
back into chilled hands and feet,
all of us wrapped in a thin
icy fog.

One of them shakes his mane once
—no threat, no offering—as we turn
and ski by snowlight now
past a still, frozen lake and down,
toward the lights of the valley.

THE TREEFROG AT LAUGHINGWATER CREEK

Late on, after the first October rains,
after the mossy boulders are littered
with the rust-brown dust of fallen needles,
after the squirrels are done,
then the lone treefrog of Laughingwater Creek
can have some peace.

I watch him venture out
from his moist spot in a cleft of rock
and cast his tiny eyes about for a fly.
The flies, those eyes know, have been gone
for weeks now,
and treefrog too feels a growing sluggishness
in his limbs. Numbly,
he watches a small circling of gnats—
too tired and stiff to jump.

Floating leaves drift past like rafts,
bob and scoot down the cobble stream
to a place called Laughingwater.
There, an old treefrog can sit out
his last few days in a deckchair of moss.
Where the afternoon sun is warm,
and bugs are served on small trays
of grass; and each evening
the gentle sound of quiet water,
laughing to itself,
carries deeper
into the slowly rising stars of winter.

MAC'S AUTO WRECKING

The two of them stood in drizzly headlight glare
out back among the dead and dying trucks.
Mac tinkering somewhere down in the yawn jaws
of a wheezing old Ford, the other guy
off to the side, with a beer:

"Now I don't care how much gas 'n oil I gotta pump into her,
so long as she'll run. Y'know, it's like fuck the debts 'n
fuck the parole; fuck the credit union . . . fuck everything!
I just want to take the old lady 'n the kids down to Disneyland
for Christmas. Y'know what I mean? *Fuck it!*
All I want's a car that'll make it down to California 'n back."

Mac
tilts his head up from under the hood,
squints one eye:

"'N *back?*"

"Widowmaker"

Only the faintest *tic*
when I set the bar of the idling saw
against the next tree,
leaned back and looked up
—then a flash—

When I came to, Burns,
the crew boss, stood
sizing me up like a downed log.
"Is it busted?"

The ground was soft with moss
and damp leaves;
a light dimpling of spring rain was
cool on my face.

I felt with gloved hand where
the limb peened off the rim
of my hardhat and clipped me
clean across the nose.
Bubbling, warmly. It was hard to tell.

What I really wanted
was for Burns
to switch off the damn saw
still idling by my ear,

and when he did
I was grateful to lie there
in the leaves and moss,
holding my nose and
lucky young life,

and let the ringing in my ears
subside
into birdsongs.

▸ 4 ▸
THROUGH HIGH STILL AIR

A Season at Sourdough Mountain

NIGHT, SOURDOUGH MOUNTAIN LOOKOUT

A late-summer sun
threads the needles of McMillan Spires
and disappears in a reef of coral cloud.

Winds roil the mountain trees,
batter the shutter props.

I light a candle with the coming dark.
Its reflection in the window glass
flickers over mountains and
shadowed valleys
seventeen miles north to Canada.

Not another light.

The lookout is a dim star
anchored to a rib of the planet
like a skiff to a shoal
in a wheeling sea of stars.

Night sky at full flood.

Wildly awake.

DAWN

Predawn is calm and still,
then the low rumble of a truck
climbing Highway 20, a mile below.

Diffused light in high cloud
gathers behind the eastern peaks,
slowly implodes into the rising sun.

At 6:30, sun clears the summit ridge
of Jack Mountain and washes the lookout
in a flood of warmth.

Tea and zazen by the open door.
Hui-neng says,
"It is that which is before you."

Hundreds of peaks and snowfields
in a dazzling circle in early light.
This "glass pagoda" at its center.

A granite basin exquisitely carved
by long centuries of starlit ice
and quiet dawns, filled with emptiness.

HAWKS

Mid-afternoon and hawks
spiral up the thermals
from Diablo Canyon—

    red-tails, Cooper's, rough-
    legs, harriers, the small
    nimble "cheetahs" of sharp-shins.

Poised, compact and gracefully alert,
(Jeffers' "intrepid readiness")
wingfeathers rippling in the updraft,

they shoot through the notch
west of the lookout
and merge into blue over
             Pierce Creek valley.

I watch with field glasses
from my mountain perch
until they vanish
         against the darker blue shadows
    of the Picket Range.

SNOWMELT

Fetching water from a small
snowmelt tarn on the ridge,
kneeling on step-stones as the pool
shrinks by the day.

Late summer of a dry year.

All around me are footprints:
    delicate tracks of
            small deer,
    nimble handprints of raccoons.
    Traces of smaller mammals—
        chipmunk and deer mouse—
all gathered
in a comradely circle of drying mud.

High winds up the Skagit
pile dark-bottomed clouds
against peaks and snowfields.
Summits to the west and south
          obscured.

Dipper and two-gallon plastic jug.

Rinse my face in a last pool
         of winter snow
as mountains gather
the first fall storm
      like an animal come to drink.

HUB OF THE WHEEL

Fingers of smoke from wildfires
reach down Big Beaver and Pierce Creek valleys
and cover the deep blue of Ross Lake
like a quilt.

The drift mingles with other smokestreams
from Ruby and Thunder creeks,
where mountains, too,
have been touched by the sky.

Smoke clouds curl around Sourdough Mountain,
where I sit in the clear blue center
of this gesture: *mudra*
        of the mountain Buddhas.

Waft of incense from a world renewed,
             forests / meadows
      rained into soil.
The teachings come round again.

THE END OF THE OCEAN

High clouds at dawn
and finger tracings of moisture
in the eastern sky.

From beyond the western rim
of mountains,
ocean's breath floods the valley.

Mist spills over high ridges.

One by one, the peaks
wink out. Soon, the lookout
is wrapped in blowing cloud.

Wetness drips from propped shutters.
The visible world
beyond misted windows,
       an isthmus of rock and heather.

       "I stood as one stupefied,"
       wrote Petrarch.
       "I looked down and saw
       the clouds lay beneath my feet.
       I felt as if
       another."

Clark's nutcracker dips from a cloud,
lights on a hemlock limb
and calls: once, twice . . .

       "No bird who flies
       knows the limits of the sky,"
       says Dogen,

"no fish who swims, the end
of the ocean."

Taste of raincloud moving past,
streams and rivers
              beginning again.

At the near edge of ocean's reach,
traces of older cycles:
weathered rock / wandering seas,

century-old hemlock scrub
              in blowing mist, black wings

. . . flaps off & disappears.

BREATH

Into the clear morning air, the radio
crackles with a med-evac call.
Sheriff's deputy from a small town
in the valley:
Street address. Time of report.
An "individual" overdosed on sleeping pills,
"still breathing."
Later, "a female, 21 years old."
She's rushed to the E.R. in Sedro Woolley.

Morning sunlight on the cliffs
and snow-blue glaciers of Colonial Peak.

Timeless beauty and human grief—
between these poles
the world's suffering wakes anew
with each striking sunrise.

CLOUDS

Late afternoon, the mountain
half clothed in blowing fog.

Dark twin summits of Hozomeen
drag at the cloud bottoms,
while the soft, sunlit slopes
                of Spratt Mountain
fold green and ivory-shored
into the quiet blue of Ross Lake.

The small wooded raft
                of Tenmile Island
drifts north with the wind,
and Ponderosa Point steps gingerly,
        ankle deep
into lakewater.

Light wind plays with the clouds.
Sunlight and shadow drape
                and undrape
the knees and thighs,
        the forest-robed lengths
    of soft undulate hills;

creek valleys
yielding to rain-damp meadows
        hidden in mist. I imagine

getting lost up there.

TROPICAL SUNLIGHT

Smoke from wildfires fills the valleys,
and a high veil of cirrus
      dampens the morning sun.
Then a gift from Costa Rican forests—
Townsend's warbler drops by.

Sunlit yellow face and breast,
dark Zorro-like mask,
quickly, neatly, shakes down
      a subalpine fir crown
for bugs,
cleans his beak madly on a limb,
and takes leave south
      across the Skagit,
         heading back.

From the lookout steps,
three thousand miles north,
I'm warmed through.

SUNSET

Late flush of evening cloudlight
glowing through old rippled window glass.

Steam curling from teacup
in cool night air.

Only the mountains are still.

Night, Diablo Lake

The lakewater is polished slate
as night moves over mountains.
A wedge of sky, pale
        and smooth as milk,
     opens to the west.

No moon tonight, but Jupiter
floats between darkened peaks,
and splinters of stars ignite
      the deepening sky.

Suddenly, from across the water
come the ululant voices of loons.

It's as if the peaks
and blue-gray waters
      have given voice to the night,
a quiescent mingling of solitude and desire.

At dark, ghostlike,
a white deer
steps from shoreline trees
     into a clearing.
In the moon's absence she carries
a muted light all her own—

planet, loon song and deer, all
of a moment that opens
      into a timeless presence—

then, slips back into the brush,
formless and incandescent as breath.

، 5 ،
THE WAY TO WINDY RIDGE

ASCENDANCE

—after a historic photograph by Ellis Morigeau

When a wild chinook thrashes the air
above Kettle Falls,
the coiled spring of its body
ripples with the surge of 700 river miles
                        toward home.

The river pours its thunder
between striate seabottom rocks:
a glassy tongue imploding into whiteness.

To the salmon it is a beckoning arm.

There is no human gesture so fervent
—this long journey inland—
no effort so seamlessly one with its element.

The river's story, descending
through epochs of ice and stone,
coalesces in the salmon's momentary flight.

The salmon's heart
is the river's heart made flesh.
The salmon's flight, a pulse.

Ours is the wisdom to see them both
as one; power to power joined:

one falling,
one borne by a wisdom all its own

        in ascendance.

AT GOBLIN GATES, ELWHA RIVER

"For several hundred feet, as far as can be seen down the
canyon, a multitude of faces appear in succession near
the water's edge. One could conceive in them a tortured
expression." —Charles A. Barnes, March 5, 1890.

Upvalley, my fire is a point of light
flickering on a gravel bar.
But here the river tightens
against a ridge of sandstone,
pools restlessly at a cliff face,
and plunges through a jagged river-cut slot
                        to a deep canyon.

Barnes called this the "Goblin Gates,"
and from just upstream
the serrated walls do present
a ghoulish aspect,
but what holds me here is the river.

Deep, slate blue, muscular
as it curls against the cliff, then
—a blade of light
splintering over a gallery of boulders—
drops away into gray-green spray
                        and distance.

A mile or so down-canyon the river
quiets beneath the flat calm
of impounded lakewater.
One could conceive "a tortured expression"
there, too.

Sky darkens over the autumn flush of maples;
my fire has fallen to a muted glow.

As I start back, the ancient forests
        of the Elwha valley rise unbroken
to distant ridgelines
where the ragged gates of treetops
unleash a flood of stars.

ON THE RESERVOIR FLOOR

On the reservoir floor with
the dam taken down,

the ghosts of the old forest
re-gather—emerged
        from lakebottom gravels,
washed free by riverflow, and
perfectly preserved.
               They are
that rarest of nature's mysteries,
        an unfilled niche; no
aquatic wood-munching organisms,
so a century later
the old stumps appear
              freshly cut.

I can feel the axe-bites
in the springboard notches,
smooth crosscut saw kerf
        of felling cuts,
sense the coolness
of deep shade beneath
leaning cedar and fir.

Glint of broken sunlight on the river
riffling blue-green over river-smooth stones,
and holding briefly
        in deeper pools

where the first intrepid steelhead
—fierce, homing spirit of tree-lined waters—
taste the freshness of river's source
again.

OPENING THE RIVER

1

Shadow and light in the moss-green canyon.
Rivershapes,
fluid and muscular beneath surface glimmer,

    spool and coil
        in the deep pool
    at the concrete foot of the dam.

Beneath painted banners and cedar boughs
Elwha Klallam dancers and drummers
lift an old song into the trees,
    into the hills beyond,
        into the sky . . .

raised hands and arms,
fringed shawls, dark flowing hair.
A celebratory song.

Old friends and allies, local politicians,
company men, officials
from both Washingtons.
Park folks in their dress greens.
Dick Goin, who carried the torch for decades.
Polly Dyer at 90.

    And the people of this river
    —of salmon, elk and cedar—
    Elwha Klallam.

The river strong and streaming through us all.

2

"Answered prayers today—all
down through the years . . .
Many of those prayers have gone up.
Many tears were shed; many lives
            cut short."
                        Ben Charles sees
his ancestors gathered around us
in the sky above the river.

"A great cloud of witnesses,
and they're all there, smiling. So many
are so happy. So many are crying."

His voice a prayer for the attendant guests.

"A hundred years is a long time to us,
but to the Creator
that's just the blink of an eye."

A blink, too,
to the silvery dark eyes of the swimmers,
—eyed eggs in gravel, cold
fluid wash of native waters—

chinook,
gliding restless in the undulant flow
            of the canyon.

The Klallam elder cries
and laughs through his tears.

"Bless this day, Creator. Bless these people.
Keep them in your hand."

3

For a century, Elwha and Glines Canyon dams
raised an impenetrable wall
to returning salmon, forest creatures
keyed to these waters
since the ice drew back, and forests
slowly returned to valley floors.

—400,000 fish: chinook, pink, coho, chum
and steelhead—

in the river's prime.

Concrete dams, penstocks and turbines
siphoned the power of clear
        rushing snowmelt
to mill then pulp the felled forests

for "peace, power and civilization."

And with the steel and concrete grip
of two mountainous fists,
choked the lives of a people.

Now, after a quarter-century effort,
the day has come when the river
at last will be free.

Sun breaks through early cloud,
brightens lichens on the limbs of trees.
Raven perches in a streamside fir,
and the river sings
        low and steadily,
strong in the canyon beyond us.

4

Officials are generous with thanks
and praise:
the agencies, the mill, the city . . . , some
who fought like hell to keep
this day from arriving.

Then, like a fresh wind from the strait,
Frances Charles rises to speak.
Small and strong,
driven as the salmon she fiercely defends,
yet deeply grateful,

she thanks her tribal elders for their faith,
asks the veterans in the tribe to stand,
and acknowledges the tribal youth—always
the future alongside the past.

"The creation site is behind you,"
gesturing over the impounded waters.
"Coiled basket" rocks
—where Creator bathed the first people
and set them here—

drown beneath a reservoir
named for the scoundrel that bullied
his dam through, regardless.

Upstream, hundreds of square miles,
whole ranges of primal forest,
home to Bear, Elk, Fisher and Winter wren,
wait for the silver pulse to return
to the salmon-starved waters,
to become again whole.

When at last Aaron Jenkins
fires up the excavator and takes
the first bite out of the check dam
a cheer and applause goes up from the crowd.
And the *Elwha,* "River of Elk,"
resumes her ancestral journey.

In less than a year,
chinook and steelhead will flash
past the rapid of the old dam site,
past the logged-off cedar stumps
and newly planted trees, past
Coiled Basket rock to Indian Creek
and Little River and the riffles
below Altaire pool—

Reaching home again,
"the deep note of our dwelling here,
the silver soul of this green bell,"

offering people everywhere
a new way to be
on this riverine, blue-green sphere
we share.

ORONDO, 1973

Decades now since we bumped north
in the back of a dusty van. Orondo,
Entiat, the small appletowns bunched
along the banks of the slack green waters
of the Columbia,
and the tawny flesh-colored hills beyond them
freckled with sage and creased with arroyos.

We hoped for a few more weeks
of harvest work, but the crop was thin
that year, and the last flatbed loads
of apple bins rumbled past us,
down 97 to the sorting yards at Wenatchee.

By Chelan, we gave it up.
A raw wind chafed over the lake,
and the deepening overcast marked an end
to the blue sunlit harvest days
and brilliant dawns of autumn.

It was late in the day, your birthday,
and we didn't know
where we would spend the night.
We didn't know a lot of things then,
but it was this—sharpened by what we both knew
about us and the end of another season—
that left you quiet and hurt.

I can't remember where we did sleep that night.
I do remember coming home
to the damp cabin and empty woodshed,
and the pain of those last weeks.

92

But left to its own, memory wanders
beyond that, to the still-green and apple-red
days of harvest, when we'd return
to our pickers' shack under the trees,
and you'd wash in a white enamel basin.

I remember your beauty as you stood
by the glimmering warmth of the gas burner
brushing leaves from your hair,
and my sadness, as our small window
darkened on the rows of neatly pruned trees
and burnt glow of the sage hills beyond them,
that I'd already lost you.

AT CAMERON PASS

—for Mike O'Connor

The scrubbed August light is falling,
and evening haze lifts from the Lost
and Elwha valleys.
Forested ridgetops and far snowlit peaks
drift in a sea of blue-gray light.

We climbed the trail from Lost Basin
but linger on the windy pass,
three of us: my wife and an old,
dear friend, one last time
before descending to camp in the valley.

All that we hold closest—
love, friendship, this small,
wild corner of broken earth—
holds us now.
Mountains and rivers lift and fall away

into the cool measured wind of the Pacific.
Through seasons to come,
this same ceaseless breath of wind,
wind of dwarf juniper,
wind of falling stars.

Breath that rolled waves
over the seabottom silts and sands
we stand on, breathing again,
briefly, through us.

We talk, laugh and share
a hurried embrace
before dropping into the calm north shadow,
in the lee of our moment here.

94

SOLITUDE

Back from a season of work
in Southeast Alaska,
Tim Roddam sat alone with his lunch
at the edge of a landing, where
I joined him.

Seventy acres of stumps,
logging slash and gullies
fell away below us.
High, mounded clouds
hurtled east on the coastal wind,
and a pair of ravens flapped west.

They *cronked* loudly overhead
as if passing judgment
on the mess we've made of things;
near enough
to hear the faint chuff
of their wingbeats.

Then from one, came a complex riff
of croaks, barks and *chirrufs* . . .
"That first one," Tim spoke up,
"is about to fly upside down."

And it did. Flapped
a few ungainly wingbeats, then
flipped back upright.

I turn to Tim, speechless.
"When I was thinning, up North
on Wrangell Island, we camped out.
Wasn't much to do," he shrugged,
"but watch ravens."

The two, by then,
had spanned the breadth of the cut
and disappeared past the far trees.

SHEEP CANYON

—for Randy & Robin

We followed cougar tracks
over wet sandbars,
up the copper-green flow
of the Escalante.

Wherever we crossed,
she had crossed, and we came
to look forward to the neat
round prints, dimpled

with last night's rain.
Above camp that night
at Sheep Canyon
Randy found the den.

Deep cave beneath
a large sandstone boulder
blue-black with lichen.
It faced east for early sun

and was pitched to shelter
from stiff down-canyon winds.
It's sandy floor, well
below the sloping hillside,

was strewn with bones:
jawbones, femurs,
bits of rib and scattered
vertebrae;

a deer skull with
spread four-point antlers
silvery dry on the
dark sand.

I stayed there until the sun
dropped through a notch
in the sandstone cliffs
and disappeared.

The night grew cold and starry.
Moonlight traced the rim
of the far canyon wall.
My own bones bundled safely

into warm clothes
on a wide, flat rock by the river,
I had almost forgotten
what it felt like to be alive.

MORNING LIGHT

An early shaft of sunlight
slants through the forest canopy
and lights a single spray
      of huckleberry.

ovalifolium: round-leaved,
with its small, half-ripe
denim-blue berries
      tastier
than the reds of the lowlands.

For a moment its leaves are cast
in perfect shadow
on the roughscaled bark
of a hemlock.

One or two are intricately
dotted with aphid holes;
others overlap in delicate tiers
and patterns of shadow and light.

The woods are quiet.
Dew lingers on spiderweb
and moss.

As the pattern shifts,
I think of Plato's shadows,
gestures and figures silhouetted
on drawn blinds,
      the formless shapes
that linger
at the portals of dreams.

And how perception slips
imperceptibly to memory:
mind to matter to mind,
as light folds back
      into the canopy
and things return to themselves
without us.

A DISTANT GOAL

"Peace is not merely a distant goal we seek . . ."

Dr. King's words buoy us
as friends gather
and children race the chilly plaza,
at the crossroad downtown.

At dusk, our candles
flicker in the wind.

Placards lift to headlight glare
as traffic slows
and stops for the light.

Brief exchanges. Waves.
Horns from passing cars.
             If only
we could stop this headlong drive to war
                      as easily.

Maeve's hands grow cold holding a banner,
and she runs off
to join the other kids.

Not merely a distant goal—
the peacemaker wrote of another war
"—but a means
             by which we arrive there."

Darkness comes on
over the smoky glow of taillights
as children a half-world away
take shelter from the night sky.

DECEPTION PASS, BEFORE THE BOMBS FALL

With Navy jets strafing the heavens,
the trees gather small intermittent silences
into themselves.

I walk out through wet winter brush.
I stop to listen to the story of a leaning cedar
as it folds its bark over an ancient burn.

Along charred heartwood
I feel the rough burnt edge of old bark,
the burgeoning growth of healthy sapwood,

as a fighter jet splits the sky.

Into the leaf's-breadth of silence
that follows, a winter wren utters
its clear, ebullient song.

Its notes pierce the darkness of war-noise
like a blossom of light, resplendent
with an ounce and a half of hope.

A Mountain Blessing

Across the high basin,
green sloping meadows and bands of rock
drop steeply to a cobalt lake.

Slow, metallic trickles ring
from withering snowbanks;
scraps of cloud dissipate,
and the mountain world is numinous
                    with light.

Last night, four bear
—small shadows
            darker than the shadowed cliffs—
emerged and prowled the ledges
and skirts of meadow,
hungry for summer-sweet berries.

We watched as they moved easily
across cliff face and hanging meadow.
The she-bear
and her cub descended a wall
of broken rock
            on invisible steps.
Another stemmed a smooth
water-worn gully
to a hidden pocket meadow
                and disappeared.

We stayed until cold and coming darkness
sent us back over rocks and hummocks
to camp.

Now,
as afternoon shadows cross the slope
and breezes ruffle the lake,
I listen for the ceramic clack
of stone on stone
and watch for those deepest of shadows
to re-emerge
from shrubby cloisters of trees.

I wait attentive and hopeful as a supplicant
for that blessing of the wild
to wash over me
            like a fine north wind,

and deepen my winter dreams.

ON FIRST ARRIVING AT QUINAULT

—with apologies to Su Tung-p'o

Funny—I never could keep my checkbook balanced,
And it gets worse the older I grow.
Low clouds wreath the hills—like a Sung scroll;
Narrow road through rain-forest trees—
                eleven inches last week alone!
Not that I mind, a seasonal laborer on the road crew;
"Other poets have worked for the water bureau."
But I worry about all the poems
              idling away in the high meadows;
Who will be there to catch them
When I'm tarring a leak inside a culvert
With July Creek sluicing down my back, and the weekend
Still days away?

WILLOW WITHES

My grandfather used willow withes
cut from a backyard shade tree
to tie back his grapevines to their arbors—
leafy rows that bordered
the other crops sewn into his small,
hillside farm.

With a bundle of cut swaths tucked in his belt
he strode the rows like a swashbuckler,
whipping wands and binding unruly growth
into order. Following along
with my armload of cut willow limbs,
I could barely keep up.

I did better with strawberries.
scooching my butt down the dusty rows,
filling my grandmother's big two-handled colander,
the taste of ripe berries erupting warmly
against my tongue.

Scooching, too, I could thin carrots
with the best of them,
grasping the lacy tops close to the soil
and tugging.
The small, fingerling carrots, rinsed
in the tublike yard sink,
crunched sweetly between my teeth.

Other days I gathered brown eggs
from the cloying henhouse,
or fed the rabbits in their shaded hutches,
or broke the ends off stringbeans
with Noni under the backyard willow,
her apron a brimming green horn-of-plenty.

Or watched plains of tomatoes ripening
on wire-mesh racks,
smoke from the summer kitchen redolent
in the fragrant air.

The green willow withes dried over summer
as the wine grapes thickened and set,
and by September, when all the family gathered
for harvest, their golden coils seemed
an organic part of the vines,

bound like memories, now
with the farm gone, shoring up the bounty
beneath yellowing leaves,
so it can be gathered,
and pressed and tasted.

Setting the glass down on the
white enamel table,
tartness waking the tongue.

My Father Speaking

In those years, the oughts and early teens,
it was woods from Mt. Pleasant Street clear
to West Peak. Eight of us kids then—
Fran wasn't born yet—and I'll be honest,
we were often hungry. We'd find food
where we could.

In fall when the chestnuts were ripe
we'd comb McCarty's woods for them.
We smaller kids would get a boost up
to the lower limbs, but
the big boys would find stout logs
and give the trees a whack. Oh brother,
would those chestnuts come showering down.

We'd fill gunnysacks, all we could carry,
and haul them back to Ma
who'd roast them in the cookstove.
The house would fill with their flavor,
the nicest, sweetest nuts you ever ate.

In 1917 the blight took them all.
They never came back.
When you were kids I'd bring home
bags of European chestnuts, remember?
But nothing, nothing compared to those wild nuts
from the woods.

To tell the truth,
I don't know what we'd have done without them.

THE COUNSEL OF PINES

When I'm weighted down with the futility
of trying to change anything,
I seek the high ridges
and good counsel of whitebark pines.

Gnarled and wind-blasted,
they spread wide, long-limbed crowns
and stiff tufts of needles
expansively
among the slender spires
of mountain hemlock and subalpine fir.

They welcome the full pitch of wind,
needle-blast of ice, slow broil
of summer sun.
They embrace their mountain world full-on.

At the highest reaches
even they are brought to their knees,
and storm-hobbled, crawl shrublike
along ridge crests, limbs
unfurled in tattered banners
against the cobalt sky.

Every now and then
I need to see that.

Along a ridge on the Cascades crest
I find the charred hulk
of a lightning-struck pine.
Its trunk shattered on talus,
its broken-off base silver-brown,
sunbaked amber, flecked

with delicate furls of wolf lichen.
But inside the charred hollow,
is the deep green of boxwood leaves,
and beside them, a single sprig
of whitebark
scrabbling up
through a rubble of ash and duff.

The Way to Windy Ridge: Mount St. Helens

*"I'm grateful to the mountain
because it gives me the opportunity to pray."*
—Ursula Le Guin

1

We follow a high ridge
from Smith Creek headwaters
through crimson paintbrush
and healing stalks of fireweed,
      bright and tossing in the summer wind.

The white cymes of *Anaphalis:*
      "pearly everlasting"
flit and swirl pollyannish
      over this momentary landscape.

First to come flocking back.

2

The trail is cut through a blowdown fir,
wide rings of growth at its heart
sprung from an earlier disturbance
            —tephra fall or wildfire—
and dense rings of the outer edge
      marking centuries of quiet growth.

Then—
      one day.

Juncos say, "Same world, Tim."

3

Below us, Spirit Lake is roofed
with a forest of drift-logs.

Continents form
        and disassemble in wind,
collide and rift apart
as restless as the larger continents

afloat
on that warmer sea
                just beneath us.

4

We skirt a palisade of lava cliffs,
remnant of an earlier flow.

Snags rise like Doric columns.
Loose rocks rumble and clack
to lakeshore;
puffs of ash float back up.

From a shallow ledge on the cliff face,
a delicate columbine blossom
        and wind-shook sprays of saxifrage
show us the way:

quiet exuberance
as the ground slips and rises beneath us.

5

Around a final shoulder of ridge
the sloped expanse of Pumice Plain
        (drift of the mountain that stood before)

112

spreads into uneasy mesas
incised
      by shifting streams.

From a distance, the pale scrim of plant life
scrabbles wildly
        over the newly born ground,
     claiming each niche and corner.

6

From the mile-wide bowl of the crater,
where dust and ash billow
from collapsing walls,
and an incipient glacier gathers itself,

the blessing of earthwarm water
spills through the blasted breach
         to a nascent greening earth
opaque with promise.

7

We stand at a windy altar.
The volcano is washed in morning light.

Just out of sight,
a new lava dome heaves and falls,
swells at a pace that staggers.

The mountain is a window,
        open
     on the moment of creation.
From its ragged skirts
a fresh and hungry world unfurls.

Sinuous canyons, brushy slopes
and high windy ridges—
where we
                    for the moment
          enter into its story.

The view from here is more powerful,
daunting, yet flush with hope
                    for this damaged earth

than anyone dared imagine.

NOTES TO THE POEMS

"Poncho in Heaven," p. 10 — Title is from a kindergarten drawing my daughter did in memory of her kitty, Poncho.

"The Pope of Swimming Bear Lake," p. 13 — Swimming Bear Lake is the unofficial name of a small alpine tarn in upper Cat Creek basin in Olympic National Park, Washington. Lake and bear appear in the film, *The Olympic Elk,* 1952.

"State Championship," p. 16 — Epigraph is from Robert Sund's poem, "Why I am Singing for the Dancer," in *Poems from Ish River Country: Collected Poems and Translations,* Shoemaker & Hoard, 2004.

"Winter Solstice, Moonrise at Century's End," p. 19 — On winter solstice, December 22, 1999, the full moon was at perigee (closest to the earth), the first such alignment in 130 years.

In the sequence "Reflected Light, Poems on Paintings by Morris Graves," titles in quotes are titles of paintings that inspired the poems. Since Graves often worked in series, some paintings share the same title. To avoid confusion, I've numbered paintings in the "Hibernation" series I through III.

"Varied Thrush Calling in Autumn," p. 26 — Some of Graves's most haunting images come from the time leading up to and during World War II. This painting was done the year before Graves's interment for conscientious objection to the war.

"Each Time You Carry Me This Way," p. 30 — Title is a re-phrasing of a line from the *Puranas* spoken by Vishnu to the goddess Earth as he rescues her from the sea.

"A Bear Comes to the Wedding," p. 45 — The poem was inspired by (and first two lines borrowed from) Howard McCord's poem "The Bear that Came to the Wedding," from *Maps*, Kayak Books, 1971.

"Widowmaker," p. 64 — Loggers' slang for a dead limb or top hidden in a tree's upper canopy.

The sequence "Through High Still Air" is from the 2003 fire season spent at Sourdough Mountain Lookout in North Cascades National Park, Washington. The title takes a line from Gary Snyder's poem "Mid-August at Sourdough Mountain Lookout" (*Riprap and Cold Mountain Poems*, Counterpoint Press, 2009). 2003 was the 50th anniversary of Snyder's stint at Sourdough lookout.

"Dawn," p. 70 — Hui-neng was the Sixth Patriarch of Chan (Zen) Buddhism in Tang Dynasty China and originator of the *Platform Sutra*. He taught that the essence of Buddha's teaching lies in what is before our eyes.

"The End of the Ocean," p. 74 — Sourdough Mountain lies at the eastern edge of the coastal Puget Sound-Salish Sea basin. Petrarch, the 14th-centry poet and scholar, climbed Mont Ventaux in Provence in 1335 and wrote about the experience. He is considered the first alpine tourist. Dogen Zenji is the 13th-century founder of Zen Buddhism and author of the *Mountains and Rivers Sutra*. Quote is from his *Shobogenzo*.

"Ascendance," p. 83 — Lower Kettle Falls on the Columbia River, now inundated beneath Lake Roosevelt behind Grand Coulee Dam.

"At Goblin Gates," p. 84 — Epigraph is from Charles Barnes of the Press Expedition, quoted in Robert L. Wood's *Across the Olympic Mountains*, University of Washington Press, 1967.

"On the Reservoir Floor," p. 86 — Lake Aldwell following removal of Elwha Dam, spring, 2012.

"Opening the River," p. 87 — Ben Charles, Sr., is an elder of the Elwha Klallam Tribe. "[P]eace, power and civilization" from Thomas Aldwell, *Conquering the Last Frontier,* 1950. Frances Charles is tribal chairperson. "[T]he deep note of our dwelling here..." is from Tom Jay, "Homecoming," in *The Blossoms are Ghosts at the Wedding,* Empty Bowl, 2006.

"On First Arriving at Quinault," p. 105 — After Su Tung-p'o's "On First Arriving at Huang-chou." Road crew, Olympic National Park.

"The Way to Windy Ridge," p. 111 — Epigraph spoken by Ursula Le Guin at Mount St. Helens, Washington, July 24, 2005.

BIOGRAPHICAL NOTE

Tim McNulty is a poet, essayist, and nature writer. He is the author of three poetry collections, including *In Blue Mountain Dusk,* and *Pawtracks,* and ten poetry chapbooks. He is also the author of eleven books on natural history, including *Olympic National Park: A Natural History,* and *Washington's Mount Rainier National Park.* Tim has received the Washington State Book Award and the National Outdoor Book Award. He lives with his wife, Mary Morgan, in the foothills of Washington's Olympic Mountains.

The text of this book is set in ITC Galliard designed by Matthew Carter in 1978 based on the 16th century designs of the French typecutter Robert Granjon. The display font is Trajan Pro designed by Carol Twombly based on the second century CE inscription at the base of Trajan's column in Rome.

Poetry by Tim McNulty available from Pleasure Boat Studio:
A Literary Press:

In Blue Mountain Dusk   ISBN 0–9651413–8–1 $13
Some Ducks   ISBN 978–1–929355–55–6 $10
Through High Still Air, Poems and Journals
     ISBN 1–929355–27–0 $9
Cloud Studies, Twenty Poems form Pawtracks
     ISBN 978–1–929355–46–4 $8

To order these and other titles directly from Pleasure Boat
Studio, visit our website at www.pleasureboatstudio.com
Pleasure Boat Studio: A Literary Press
201 West 89th Street
New York, NY 10024
Tel / Fax: 8888105308
www.pleasureboatstudio.com / pleasboat@nyc.rr.com

Tim McNulty's website is timmcnultypoet.com